Nature's Footprints

IN THE
BARNYARD

By Q. L. Pearce and W. J. Pearce

Illustrated by Delana Bettoli

Silver Press

For my mother
Thelma Rosalyn
—D.B.

10 9 8 7 6 5 4 3 2 1

Library of Congress Cataloging-in-Publication Data

Pearce, Q. L. (Querida Lee) Nature's footprints in the barnyard / by Q. L. Pearce and W. J. Pearce; pictures by Delana Bettoli. p. cm. Summary: Briefly describes the behavior of such domestic animals as the rooster, pig, sheep, and duck. 1. Domestic animals—Juvenile literature. [1. Domestic animals.] I. Pearce, W. J. (William Julian), 1952-   II. Bettoli, Delana, ill. III. Title.
SF75.5.P4 1990
636—dc20
89-39508
CIP
AC
ISBN 0-671-68828-6   ISBN 0-671-68824-3 (lib. bdg.)

A Note to Parents

NATURE'S FOOTPRINTS is a read-aloud picture book series that introduces children to a wide variety of animals in a unique, interactive way.

Ten animals are presented in pairs, along with a sample of each animal's footprints. In the scene that follows, the animals can be found by tracking the paths of their footprints, thereby building your child's observational skill in a lively, fun format.

Detailed illustrations and text provide more information about the animals. Encourage your child to point out details about the animals and their environment.

Accompanying the NATURE'S FOOTPRINTS series is the NATURE'S FOOTPRINTS FIELD GUIDE—a handy, colorful reference guide that teaches children even more about the animals in this series.

THE ROOSTER

Cock-a-doodle-doo!
The rooster crows.
It is morning on the farm.

THE COW

Mooooo!

Cows give us milk in the morning.

Then they go out to the sunny meadow.

The rooster eats corn in the barnyard.

Follow nature's footprints.

They will lead you to the colorful rooster.

The cow eats grass in the meadow.
Follow nature's footprints.
They will lead you to the hungriest cow.

THE HEN

Cackle-cackle-cackle!

The noisy hen gives us eggs.

There are lots of hens in the barnyard.

THE PIG

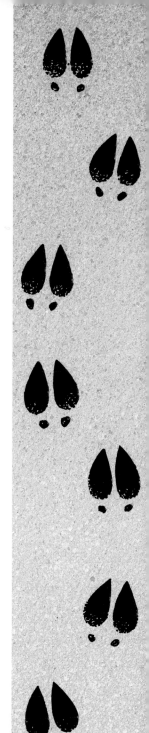

Oink! Oink!

From the plump pig comes bacon and pork.

The pig enjoys a cool roll in the mud.

Baby hens are called chicks.

Follow nature's footprints.

They will lead you to the hen with the most chicks.

Baby pigs are called piglets.

Follow nature's footprints.

They will lead you to the pig with the biggest piglet.

THE SHEEP

Baaa! Baaa!

We get wool from the sheep's fluffy coat.

The wooly coat is clipped in spring.

THE DOG

Woof-woof!

The dog barks at the sheep to make them move.

The dog barks to frighten other animals away.

The sheep stay together in a flock.
Follow nature's footprints.
They will lead you to a lost sheep.

The dog protects the flock.
Follow nature's footprints.
They will lead you to the busy dog.

THE HORSE

Neigh! Neigh!

The horse is a helpful animal.

The horse gives the farmer a ride on its back.

THE GOAT

Maaa! Maaa!

The goat gives us milk.

Goat's milk is used to make cheese.

The horse likes to run.

Follow nature's footprints.

They will lead you to the fastest horse.

The goat likes to jump.

Follow nature's footprints.

They will lead you to the playful goat.

THE DUCK

Quack-quack!

The duck gives us eggs.

The duck swims in the pond.

THE HOUSE CAT

Meow! Meow!

The house cat catches pesty mice and rats.

The house cat is the farmer's friend.

At night the duck sleeps in the barnyard.

Follow nature's footprints.

They will lead you to the sleeping duck.

At night the cat hunts for mice in the barn.

Follow nature's footprints.

They will lead you to the hunting cat.